JOHN

THE

REVELATOR

URBANCIK

JOHN
THE REVELATOR
URBANCIK

For more information, please visit www.darkfluidity.com

ISBN-10: 1-951522-00-1
ISBN-13: 978-1-951522-00-1 (DarkFluidity)

DEDICATED TO
THE MEMORY OF
MARY "MERY-ET" LESCHER

I MISS YOU

Who's
that
writing?

JOHN

THE

REVELATOR

URBANCIK

It started on a Sunday.
Could've been any day,
    but I was resting.
On a Sunday, I was resting,
    and I saw a thing,
           a vision,
           something I could not understand.
I didn't see the paths.
    I only saw the ends
           the seals
           the chaos.
It started on a Sunday
    in the swamps of New Orleans,
    and I cried.

A wind comes from somewhere.
    It doesn't simply start
    all on its own.
    I blame the flapping
    of little wings, like sparrow wings
    and hummingbirds,
    and the exhalations
    of a thousand babies
    in the city.

    Vastly
    outnumbered
    and outgunned,
    but not
    outsmarted.

I didn't know what would or even might happen.
I was a kid.
In my experience,
spell work and Ouija boards were
made by Parker Brothers.
And in all fairness
to the thirteen year old version of me,
it appeared to be
just an ordinary deck of playing cards.
I dealt out a ten of hearts,
a king of clovers,
a queen of diamonds,
an ace of spades.
I wasn't working on a royal flush, just a straight.
But the fifth card out was a
rogue of swords,
and that's when all the trouble began.

He walks the roads
and sings the songs
and pays good money,
    real silver dollar coins,
    for every soul he picks.

Promises broken,
Vows shattered,
Trust withered,
Knives drawn,
Blood spilt,
Lives lost,
Vengeance achieved,
And all the seeds for a sequel
sown.

> Show me what a night
> on the town is really like.

Have you captured
lightning in a bottle?
Held it? Kept it?
Waited for a
sunny day to
let it loose?

Dance
is a
natural
state

There
must be
an answer.

She made a thing. The thing grew wings

and became terrifying. The thing with the wings

would go out on a Wednesday to the wing shop

and get BBQ sauce and terrify the servers

and the hostess and all the other diners,

but not the line cook.

The line cook had a chef's knife.

The line cook was not afraid.

So the line cook and the thing with wings

became the best of friends and, on Wednesdays,

cruised the town for ladies.

The garden occupies an alley between two brick buildings on a stark corner of the city. Sometimes, you'll find brick dust on the flower petals, but those flakes seem to belong. It adds texture to the colors in a most agreeable way.

It isn't the oldest section of the city, but that can be argued. It is definitely old, no matter how you judge it, and the garden is old, and the flowers bloom regularly just as they have since before your grandmother was young.

All the maps, the plans and plats and blueprints of the city, show an alley just like any of the others. No city officials tend the garden. They won't even acknowledge it exists. Yet the roots of this garden are the roots of the city, twisting beneath the bricks and the mortar, under the ghosts of cobblestones and gas lights. You can see them in the ceilings of the subways and the walls of basements.

Blue police lights flash in the garden, but the cops don't enter and the cops don't explore. Another young lover has been lost to the city, another lover last seen alive receiving a flower picked from this very garden, another sacrifice to gods of asphalt and glass.

The city may be a bit stronger now, and it will persist a day longer, at least until somebody asks about the garden, about its red, red flowers and its tangled roots – and about all the bones tangled up within them since before your grandmother was young.

The Secret Life
of Dolls

A combination of
fiction and
nonfiction?

Rag Dolls

Jointed Dolls

As a *Guys and Dolls* thing

Not like Chucky.

Silver Lake is named for the color of the moon reflecting on its surface on a brisk winter night.

The Wolves of the Winter howled in the distance and we made camp in sight of the shore.

We knew about the wolves, had been running from the wolves and defending ourselves from the wolves since the White Season fell upon us.

The surface of Silver Lake looked wet though it was thoroughly frozen, but we didn't dare risk it under the pale moonlight.

We didn't know what might be under the ice.

We didn't know if it was hungry.

We only knew the wolves behind us.

Ah. You.
Finally.
I was
beginning
to think
I'd never
find you.

13

Thirteen people,
Thirteen clocks,
A baker's dozen,
An unlucky number,
A coven.

She was a pro.
Worked the Vegas circuit.

When she dealt the cards,
everybody knew the odds were stacked
in her favor.

Everyone knew, but the thing of it was –
she was beautiful and dangerous and alluring,
so nobody cared.

The house always won,
and every last damned one of them
believed they might curry her favor.

In the end, even I thought it,
or at least hoped for it –
if not her true favor,
if not her love or devotion or admiration,
at least a credible facsimile of it.

That's what she sold,
what she traded,
what she dealt in:
masks.

Those who fight cancer and its symptoms,

who face the torment

of a body in revolt,

no matter the type

and regardless of its remissions,

who bravely fight

or gracefully accede,

who deal with the pain –

they are heroes,

of the grandest sort,

and when Death inevitably finds them –

as Death eventually finds all of us –

these heroes will be escorted

to Valhalla.

On a rocketship,
there's no room for conflict.
There's no room for water,
where the hell are you going to store
angst and resentment?
Yet here we are,
half a galaxy away from earth,
with one dead crewman
and six suspects.

We collected our collections –
cards, dice, comics, hearts –
and surrendered them
to our new overlords.
They laughed at us, mostly,
but wanted to know
who among us
had been keeping
the hearts of our enemies
in mason jars.

EYE CANDY

Catch the moon in a net, drag it down to earth, see what else got caught up with it.

You look at the heels on those boots and you think how can she possibly walk in those things, and then you think I just don't want her walking away from me.

I can be ice.
Solid.
Absolute.
Eternal.

The winds rise and the ocean roars and the moon tucks away behind those thunderclouds, and you just know something special is coming to the shore tonight.

Her name is Anabel Lee.

"Do you want me dumb and pretty? Because I can give you that. I can give you that every day for the rest of your life, and I can make you hate it, detest it, loathe it to the core."

EYE CANDY

Year 9

The city's still on fire.

No idea what's fueling those flames.

Never been that close.

I assume some variation of sulfur

and honest hellfire.

At night, it lights all the clouds

orange and red.

And there are always clouds

because they're actually smoke.

It's cold in mid-summer now because

we haven't seen the sun since

Zero Hour.

But the car's gassed up,

the ammo hot and heavy

and anxious to eat some flesh.

I'm going demon hunting.

On the long path
        to wherever it is you're going,
                don't stop
                just because it seems tough.
        But do stop
                at least sometimes
                        to check out the flowers.

This is going to be a bumpy ride.

Where do you think you're going?
                Someplace else.
Anyplace else?
                Someplace better.
Where do you think you'll find better?
                Anywhere else.

The path to Midnight –
    ah,
    but what can I say?
        You run
        you hide
        you slip
        you fall
    You make the wrong turn
        at the wrong time
    then welcome,
        one and all!
But the path from Midnight
        is naught but tears
        and maybe death.
    Judging by the crows,
        maybe not even that.

VELOCITY

the universe
is constantly in motion

the earth is never twice
in the same space

the planet is a ship
hurtling seemingly out of control
through a vast void
filled with
everything.

the earth is a ship
which feeds us
nourishes us
keeps us
and
protects us

MATHEMATICAL VECTORS CALCULATING GRAVITY

I have always believed in
the moon. I have often seen
her in the sky looking down on me.

Beware the dancer
under the moon
for she
might
bring
great
joy
or she
might
bring great
despair.

Do not
trust the moon
when she
lies.

Motion Pictures:
An illusion reinforced with a soundtrack.

Are you bold enough
to risk everything
on a dream?

But the choice
in this world
as it is
is either
enter the game
and make enough
money
to live
within the
structure
of rules
you didn't write
and that
do not
benefit you,
or don't
and die.

THE 4 BEAUTIES

All thing and all people
are capable of great beauty.

Some people are convinced
this is not true, that they have
no beauty.

Some people embrace their
ugliness instead.

Beauty
is in
the eye of
the beholder.
Be the beholder
who beholds
beauty.

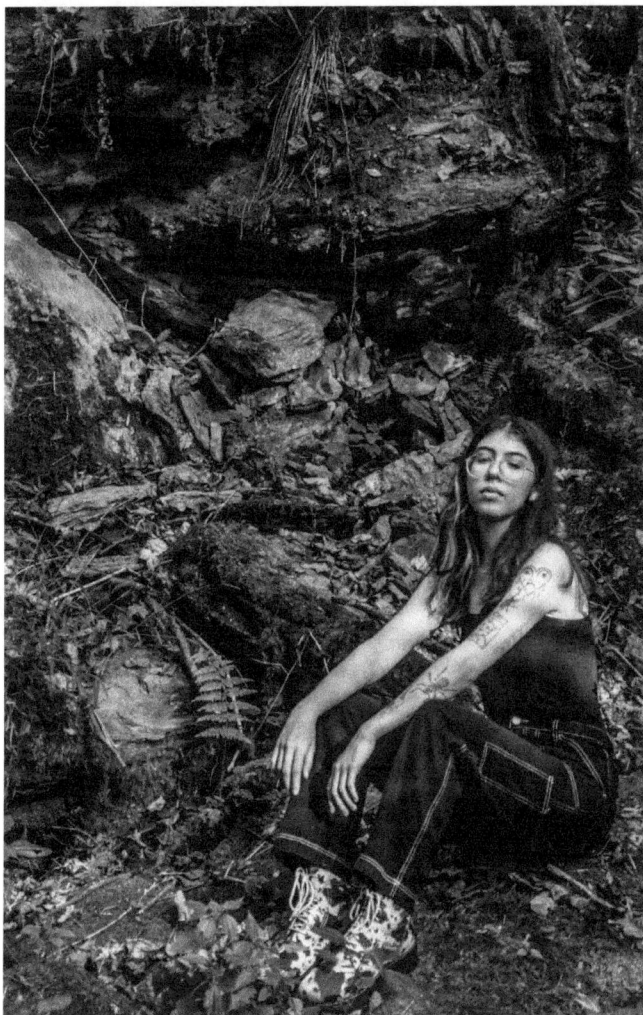

In Greek mythology,
   the winds are gods.
   The children of gods.
   Powers unto themselves.

Today, we have hurricanes.

Are hurricanes the maddest,
   Least sane of the winds?
   Or the most dedicated?

The Face of the Clock
is astronomical and
alchemical
iconography.

the wind
carries
secrets
because
everyone
tells the wind
everything

An old coin
from a distant land
traded for a favor
yet to be named.

A coin
marked   spare
with the   a few
head of a   coppers?
dragon.

Forged by a dragon.

On a flight
from one place you knew
to another, unknown place
existing in a different time,
where they speak another language,
you become the Outsider
you always feared.

I'll trade you one thousand words for a picture.

The man with the knife
knows the importance of time.
He waits until the moment is
perfect,
then sets to cutting.
Not before.

The first story was of man versus nature,
possibly a cat, possibly a storm.
The second story was a romance
with complications.

                                    The wolves howl
                              and the war starts.

There are stories, so many stories,
that aren't mine to tell.
But I'll send you to them,
to the places where you'll hear them,
because you need to know
about those stories.   tick
                                        tock
                                        tick
                                        tock

Do you trust a man
with lead pellets in his hand
and promises of great riches
on his tongue?

Am I unleashing something dangerous?
        Not dangerous. Unpredictable.

                    Even
                after set
                    down on a map,
                        the course of
                            the river
                            will change.
                        Time refuses
                    the river rest.
                We shouldn't rest
                        either.

Once upon a time,
no one knew
where a road
might take you,
not even the road itself.
Then men came along
with their maps
and said this road
goes only to this place.
But the maps lie
and change.
And the roads
have minds of
their own.

City of Bones

Do they bury their dead
out of respect
or fear?

Spell casting in the old style is rare anymore.
Today, you mostly find illusionists
playing at magic
or conjurers
pretending at necromancy
when instead their skills
lie in pulleys and ropes and
smokes and ventriloquism.
A true artist is difficult to find.
Not impossible.
Merely difficult –
and probably dangerous.

ANIMATION

the art of
the illusion of life
        No. Too restrictive.
the illusion of movement.
A dance of lines
    and colors and sound
    (both added later)
Is any art form
    so easy to define?
Through the quick
    succession of frames
    two dimensional drawings
    (and three dimensional renderings)
    are made to appear
    as if alive, capable
    of movement and life,
    defined as liveliness
    rather than breathiness.
It is a form of magic
    and maybe another trick
    meant to confound
    the senses,
or merely meant
    to excite them.

A travelling magician brings
tricks to amuse and delight,
but also promises of deeper,
heavier, more consequential
things that cannot properly
be called tricks.

at night
under
moonlight
they whisper
of a legend.

do not get lost in the glow of the night

> glowing
> colors
> dance
> as they
> fall from
> the sky

Beware
her eyes,
they'll trap you
and keep you.

SECRETS
HISTORY
MYTH
LEGEND
LANGUAGE
STORIES
WHISPERS

FOUR
    ESSENTIAL
        ELEMENTS

Magic
Mystery
Romance
Passion

Flowing through my veins
        your veins
             like blood.

A RIDE BEYOND TWILIGHT

I came upon a hut made of sticks twisted around each other to make walls and windows and enough of a doorway I could squeeze through without stabbing myself. Inside, I found more of the same: sticks, wrapped round each other to form sculptures: a dancer and a bull and a sickle moon.

Awed, maybe a little frightened, certainly mystified, I nearly believed I was imagining it when I heard the musicality of a woman whispering my name.

Her voice sounded exactly like what a man dreams of hearing under a midnight moon, all honey and bourbon promises, but something about the situation lent her voice a menacing edge difficult to describe.

I admit I froze. I have a tongue and can use it when appropriate, but just then I could conjure no words, not even a breath.

I felt her whisper at my ear when she said it again, my name, plain as day and just as simple, but she said it with intention and a strong undercurrent of possession.

Though I spun, I caught only the barest glimpse of her shadow and the echo of her giggling. I knew then the danger I was in, and I muttered half-formed curses as I narrowed my eyes against the stark of twilight.

I have seen dusk saturate the world in a golden amber hue, giving vibrancy to the greenery and thickness to the very air. This was not like that at all. It was barren, dry, cracked, and lifeless. All color was drained and subdued. When I found courage to speak – not found so much as manufactured and faked – I said, "Show yourself." I said, "Who are you?" And I said, "What do you want?"

If I had the strength or the wisdom I would've gotten back on my bike and ridden away as fast as that vintage Indian could take me. Instead, I stood there, as if awaiting an actual answer, as if expecting any response would be sane and comprehensible. But this was not the start of a conversation. This was no innocent flirtation. Names are powerful things. I'd asked for hers. Demanded it. She already knew mine. She knew my weaknesses and my strengths. She knew my hopes and fears. She knew the color of my dreams, and she would rob me of them as casually as picking a pocket.

I stood in the hut of sticks, my anger dead as driftwood.

Behind me. No, behind me again, off to one side or another. I closed my eyes and stopped trying to see her. Whatever beauty my mind applied to her, painted over her like make-up and glamour, would do more to tempt me than her terrible visage. Surely, she matched the atmosphere, the pallor and coarseness of the world about me. Her lips would not be lush and red, her hair not long and cascading like liquid amber. Her flesh would be neither soft nor supple, and would not invite touch the way her voice so masterfully implied.

Night arrived. The starkly blanched countryside was blanketed in ebon death shrouds. A chill tickled my bones.

And she kissed me.

She kissed me like a lover, deep and thoroughly, from the skin to the soul. I felt my strength, my substance, slipping into her mouth, but I was unable to resist. In her kiss, I tasted the seven sisters of the Pleiades and the dust of the Sahara and the sweetness of a good Italian prosecco with a million bubbles in every bottle. The scents of cinnamon and vanilla and cherry lip gloss overwhelmed me. In my mind, with my eyes shut tight, I could see the crystalline forests of a distant planet being flung between a pair of binary stars. I fell into her as if into a black hole.

Then she was gone, and I was on my back staring up at familiar constellations. A star fell. No, a meteorite fell, a rock no bigger than my fist, but it brightened half the night sky. An actual star fell, so distant it must have fallen a thousand years ago.

I struggled to catch my breath, to sit upright, to crawl out of the hut of sticks. I can't say why I'm still alive, but I'll never fully regain myself. A piece of me is forever lost, stolen away, leaving a shredded tattered chasm under my ribs.

I'm able to whisper a name, her name, which maybe she never meant to reveal. And it's your name. But you'll never answer.

At a ticket stand
I purchase one entry.
That's all they'll allow.
What if I want more?
You can wait
until the end
and you'll see what happens.
In the meantime,
here's a funnel cake.
And the ride
is a dark ride
without emergency exits.
There's only one way out,
a light at the end,
but what if it's a lie?
It's already swallowed
all these people I loved
and still I go around
in the dark surrounded by
Styrofoam demons and ghosts.

MOUNTAIN DANCE

Some days, the mountains hide.
When the sky is blue and the clouds crisp,
I can see the snow on every jagged rock
atop those mountains. But when the rain moves in
and the sky goes gray, I imagine the people
living in the mountains are dancing so hard,
so frenetically, they're kicking up so much of that snow,
they obscure the mountains. And maybe on those days,
the people in the mountains can't see me.
So on rainy days, cloudy days, hazy days,
I strip off all my clothes and dance in the valley.
I dance to match the rhythm of the mountains,
to compensate for any changes they might be affecting,
to provide balance to the grand order of the universe.
This, this and my red hair, is why the other
people of the valley call me a witch.
But they let me dance.
They fear the mountain people more.

the doll
stares watches witnesses
with a
glassy
eye
she
never
judges
yet she
never
loves.

An honest man
might lie
if he believes in it.
A dishonest man
never believes.

Is this what
you've always wanted?

"Just one more bottle
after this one,
and I should be okay,"
he says again.

I got to the house before anyone else, found the key behind a bell, and let myself in. The house was nice and had a basement. I knew better than to explore. It sat on the edge of a peninsular jutting into the lake. The sun was lower than the horizon but not quite down, merely hidden by trees, casting a pale silvery sheen over the water and across the sky. The waters were still. The sounds of civilization failed to reach me. I heard only Canadian geese honking somewhere across the lake, crickets, and the gentle sounds of something slipping into and out of the water. The silver shifted to gold as the sunlight dwindled, and then I was alone in the dark on the edge of water.

Some people might appreciate alone time like that as a chance to think. But I have no problem thinking. I think too much. I'm always thinking. To be honest, it gets in the way. So I welcomed this opportunity to look out over calm waters, to listen to basically insects and birds, and to shut off the thinking. It doesn't work often, but this time, it did. For a moment, it was me and nature, alone in the fresh, unspoiled night.

Then headlights came down the path, toward the lake and the house, toward me. Everyone else was arriving, and I wouldn't have another moment alone again, not like this, until I got back in my car to leave.

I was born
on an isolated island
you have to pay to visit
but might never escape alive.

there's
a void,
an emptiness,
an absence
indefinable
where
my ghost
should be.

The roads around here
twist violently,
rise and fall like movie stars,
and cling perilously close
on either side
to stone walls
and bottomless chasms
into eternity.

The train moves slowly but brings them unerringly to their destination. That doesn't mean any of them want to disembark. They didn't choose this place; they merely chose the vehicle.

The plane moves more quickly and skips huge swaths of the journey, but that doesn't mean they learn less. They might touch down anywhere at all.

The automobile tricks them into thinking they have control. But roads cannot be trusted. Trucks cannot be trusted. Their sense of direction might be askew. Untethered, they might never reach a destination.

Perhaps it would be better just to walk. How many miles did you say were left to go?

A balloon
floating
drifting
and gone.

Tie a string
before you enter
the Labyrinth,
but it won't
save you
from
the Beast.

feel
act
how I should   don't tell me how
think
dream

It's getting
harder
to breathe.

tumbling down a rabbit's hole
dreaming of adventures like Alice's
you merely twist your ankle.

                          On another world
                          they've mastered
                          the art of art
                          so that everything
                          is precise and perfect
                          and mechanical.
                          We're still messy
                          and uncertain,
                          and that
                          gives me hope.

          desperate times
        desperate measures
         haphazard results

A thunderstorm brews gray
on the horizon
and I see nothing else.

I paid an alchemist
to fill a mason jar
with a breeze
carrying the scent
of your perfume.

And in my jealous heart
I murdered him
so I could keep you
to myself alone.

I would wrestle
gods of thunder
and war
just to share
one breath
with you.

I'd offer to bring
wine, roses, and jewels –
but that's too much romance.

Blade, poison, or lies,
kill me softly
and with care.

I remember after a hurricane
and all I had was an old axe
to clear a path.
I worked all day
bathed in sweat, broiled by sunlight,
and I took a cold shower
because there was no hot water.
Then I read by candlelight
and skipped dinner
because there was nothing to cook
and no way to cook it,
and I went to the movie theater
just to sit in an air conditioned room.

la luna   la luna
le rêve   el sueño

a little bit of magic
after the lights go down
and no one will notice
the difference
if we all plays our parts
with glee.

there's a mystery
waiting to be discovered
but not solved.
A mystery solved
really isn't anything.

romance is a verb,
and when used correctly
can lead to wondrous places,
but it's also
a state of mind
and an attitude
and a philosophy.

people think passion
is just about sex,
but those are
the least passionate
people in the world.

I lost my heart in Madrid
and she's never coming back to me.
I can drink all the chocolate
and the red wine.
I can eat patatas bravas
until the thought of paprika
cracks my brain,
but I can never see
the things we didn't see together
without remembering
we never saw them.

The cat waited at the door for me
when I was far away.
He would paw at it and
make the softest mewling sounds
until I returned,
whether from overseas
or the grocery store.
The cat waits at the door now
and I cannot console him.

I don't have to know
the things you want me to know.

if I could but
touch your lips with mine,
or better,
if you would but
touch my lips with yours.

One time,
I answered the door
wearing a towel
still wet from the shower
when two women
sharing the only word they knew
came knocking.
In a parallel world,
perhaps I invited them in
and shared a word of my own.

a face in the window
fingernails tapping
on the glass
but I live
on the fifth floor
so I turn over
and return to
better dreams.

I met a woman once
and listened to her song.
It brought me to tears.
We shared stories and wine
until dawn broke again.
She hit the road
for another gig,
maybe Nashville,
maybe New Orleans,
but I was too afraid
to leave my job.

I dreamt once of the seas
and all those lost civilizations.
On the edge of the ocean
with sand sucking at my toes
I told Poseidon and the squid
and all the mermaids
I was ready to swim.

Girl Versus Poseidon

Brilliant
but too brief

Lightning cracked the sky,
dancers paused and broke the rhythm,
the ocean swallowed the shore,
and under such camouflage,
fairies like fireflies escaped.

the echo haunts
the old house
and the old man,
just the sound
of himself
spending youth.

She wanted to run away
from a Reality she couldn't face.
She wanted to make shadow puppets
dance and children smile.
I wanted to give her everything
she wanted, but I never could.

Do you want a story?
I can do that. I'm obliged to do that.
I'm a storyteller. I don't have a choice.
It's not merely a job, but an imperative.
All I've got is the stories.
The futures.
The endings.

it was a night
quiet
dark
foreboding
only the headlamps
providing light
and the radio
providing rhythm
but as fast as I pushed
the little Mustang,
I couldn't shake
the thing pacing me
in the corn fields.

Action!
Cut!
Again!
Let's see some true motivation this time.

I'm not sad
she's gone,
I'm sad about
the things
we'll never do.
I grieve for
what still awaited
in a future
now fallen
to dust and ashes.

It's not a vision,
not a flicker,
not even a ghost.
It's a memory
dancing in the shadows
tricking you,
frightening you,
reminding you.

Winter falls.

The modern
lottery:
who sits
next to you
on the plane,
train, or bus?

A new city,
a new name,
a fresh past.

Secrets
come
to me
to die.

Delight
or Delirium,
it's all the same.
Leave the bourbon bottle
please.

Through the darkness of earthy tunnels
the beast slithered and slid,
its split tongue slicing the air
to get a taste of its surroundings.
Venom dripped from its teeth,
leaving a furrow in its wake,
and once or twice it mewled,
an agonized and agonizing sound
that shattered glass and ear bones.
Only one man could face this scaled thing
and emerge victorious and still alive,
one man pantherish in his speed and agility,
one man born to barbaric ways
with sinewy thews and bluefire eyes.
But he belongs to another storyteller,
so this tale must end with
only dark triumph and despair.

The Secret Recipe
for Making Secrets:

One part shadow,
Two parts whispers,
A splash of vermouth,
and a long, thin blade

with perhaps a lemon rind garnish.

Returning
to the place,
to the memory of a place,
is like a dream
wherein everything is familiar
but you're wearing
someone else's shoes.

        No number of dollars
        no truckfull of prayers
        can undo the alchemical reaction
        of death.

     Standing at the edge of the earth
     gazing down into a horrible abyss,
     our hero valiantly swallowed his fear
     and leapt. Why delay the inevitable?

You're not half so wicked
as you pretend to be,
and I'm not
half so good.

What do you do
when "until death"
is in the past?

A wind
A wolf
A lonely cabin
and winter's
first storm
coming.

I thought once
I might like to kiss you,
and you looked at me
and caught my best smile.
I must've been wearing
some high octane glamour.
Nothing else explains
how I got you.

There was no note,
no final goodbye,
no promise of
another life
after this one.
There were only
ashes in the ocean
and salt in my eyes.

What about a dream?
Can I see you in my dreams?

Bourbon and jazz
and maybe a stranger
with red hair and a mischievous streak,
please.

At the gates
near twilight
the messenger
arrives
on the back of a
smoky steed
claiming
to have escaped
Hell itself
ahead of
advancing
armies.

She hides
in the Rain
and steals
the passing fancy
of strangers.
She slips
through the Shadows
and steals
their whispers, breaths, and dreams.
She dances
in the Moonlight
and brings
every treasure she's found
to me.
She keeps me
in this chamber
behind locks
afraid I might escape
and become again
a Stranger.

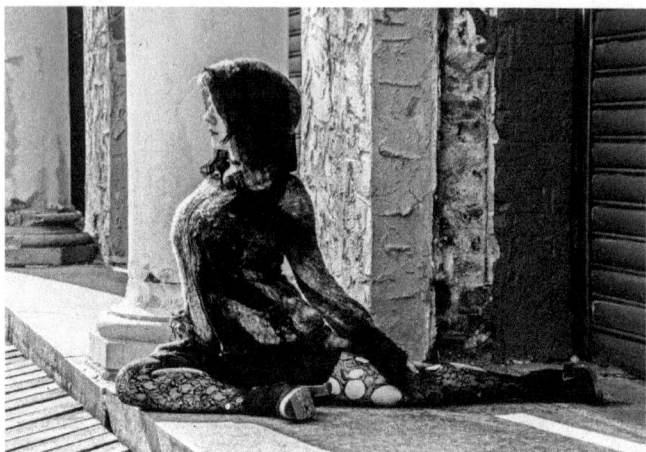

I don't
remember
all I've seen,
but I
remember
so much.

Do not
believe
the lies
no one's
told you.

Sometimes
a line or two
is all you get,
a splash of poetics,
the hint of a moon
echoed in the weather
or the paint
or the color
of her eyes.

A raven in the snow stares at me, challenging me, so I have no choice but to brave the weather with my axe hanging loosely from my hand. "What news?" I ask the bird, "brings you this far north?"

The raven flies away, further northward, beyond this stone keep at the edge of the northern world, bringing its portents to somebody else.

The raven is gone, and with it the sun finally slips under the horizon so far to the west. The long night will last a month or more.

Further north, where nothing lives but beasts and legends, there is a light. A beacon. A bad omen.

I put on my furs and wake my horse and tell her it'll be a long ride deep into the night, to the maw of winter herself. Stars streak across the sky as we ride. We make camp when the wolves sound most distant. For a stretch, the world glows green under the aurora.

Finally, I reach the palace of winter, where snow leopards mourn and the natives, not unlike men, eye me suspiciously. I stride up the aisle to where the queen lays in state, her lips blue, her skin icy, her breath gone.

I place a white rose on the glass casket and whisper my final vows. When I turn to face the mourners in the hall, I do not raise my axe. Instead, I return the way I came. I will not dishonor the fallen queen with bloodshed. And none dare follow me out.

Relax
and wait your turn,
says Death
with her scythe
and a smile.
I'll get to you
eventually.

Lightning breaks the sky
and the bits fall
with the tenderness
of rain.

Thunder rumbles
in the distance
behind me,
and the road
stretches straight
to the horizon.
It's early
in the day,
but time
for me to roll.
I wish
we could've had
another day
but these things
aren't up to me.

I'm one breath away
from kissing you.

Eyes blue as dreams.
Eyes blue as knives.
Eyes blue as summer.
Eyes blue as midnight rain.
Eyes blue as heartbreak.

Don't look too long
at her lips
or you might want
to kiss them,
and Romance
can be a dangerous thing
on a Saturday night.

It's just you
and the darkness
until the sun scratches
up from the abyss.

You were never meant
to be alone.
You will always
be haunted.

Darkness
and bourbon
are your only
companions
at 3am.

BREATHE

Eloquence
does not equate to
certainty.
It just
sounds good.

I need a distraction.

In a hole on the side of a volcano
I met Pele.

She takes on any of three forms
when visiting mortals:
the elderly woman,
the dog,
or the gorgeous young woman whose very image
has inspired a hundred generations of dreams.

I met the old lady.

She told me a story about a previous eruption
and how red hot embers rained down upon her.

In my dreams,
these embers burn away the disguise
to reveal the younger Pele as
a Phoenix awaiting rebirth.

She would have been young,
the year she told me about.

I took it as a warning
that she was ready to cast off her current face
and rise again from the ashes of herself.

That reminded me
rebirth does not belong
exclusively to the gods.

The illusionist
made a living
making women
disappear,
but he desperately
wanted to keep
just one.

Don't talk to me
of sparrows,
you freak.

Listening
to the drums
of the moon,
one realizes
you cannot evade
eternity forever.

One stroke of the brush
changes the canvas
irrevocably.

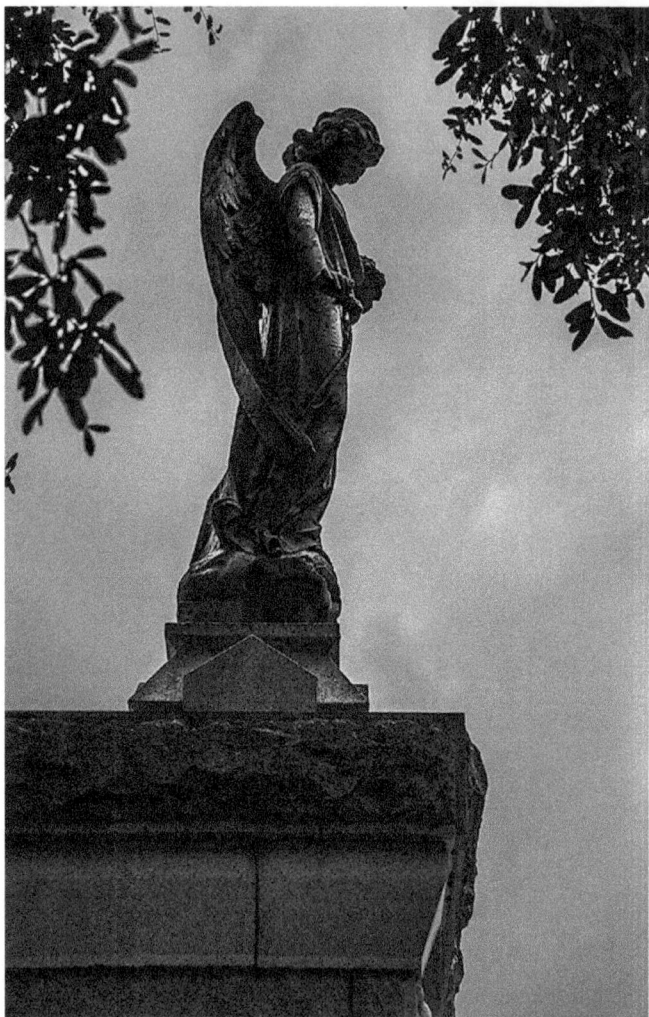

I have seen fire
sweep across nations.
I have seen waters rise
to topple skyscrapers.
I have seen the oceans at war,
and the rains,
and the locusts, one million strong,
devouring grown men and beasts
with scissor-like legs
and razor teeth
and acidic blood.

I watched helplessly as a monster
of charcoal and oil
spread through my lover's body
and left her writing in pain.
The morphine sleep
swallowed her whole.
Doctors struggled
to make it make sense.
The pestilence defied explanation.
They spun explanations at me anyway.

Why can't you see me
the way I see you?

It's hard to keep
the world balanced
underneath my feet,
but I do my best
to keep it up in the air,
floating and dancing
for the audience.

There's no magic spell
to bring my true love to me.
I've tried them all.
You're still not here.

I need a potion
to make you
fall in love
with me

or a spell
to make me
fall out.

As a butterfly, brief but beautiful,
you dance across golden fields in the dying light of day.
There are dragonflies, too, feeding on mosquitos,
and humans sipping margaritas. It's getting hard to
keep everything straight when you're sure,
once upon a time, you were able to transform.
Memory is fleeting for a butterfly, so maybe
you've forgotten how to change back.
But when you hear the newscasters,
you think maybe it's better this way,
even if life is fleeting.

A feather,
an ice cube,
a cat-o-nine tails.

A bottle of bourbon
and some old jazz records.

I have
quite the night
planned
for you.

If you make me
a promise,
I'll promise
to make you
keep it.

I do not
believe in
unhappy
endings.

You have
never been
as alone
as you've
left me.

You wouldn't know madness
if it tied you up
with silly string
and read you stock quotes
while wearing
Spider-man Underoos.

I have been conquered.
Do what you will with me.

I am a vast cauldron of passion,
a hopeless devotee to romance,
an adept of magic,
and a solvable mystery.

Alone
in a Paris café
– is this sad?
– or is this
   the promise
   of as yet
   undreamt
   romantic
   potential?

Given a hundred dreams
   a thousand
   a million
I only want
   this
   one.

If I can balance a girl
    wearing black and white stockings
    on my knees
    in the dark
    after a shot of bourbon,
I'm pretty sure
    I can handle anything.

Two clocks
in adjoining rooms
tick off the seconds.
I am paralyzed
between them,
trapped
in a stereophonic
time bomb,
able only to look
from face to face
with my eyes,
counting the staccato,
waiting
for your rescue.

You and I
are made of
stardust
and
dragon's breath,
so nothing
can kill us.
Nothing.

I'm haunted by the ghost of you
still lingering in my soul
and it's only been an hour
since we kissed.

I collect poisons
    like other people
    collect stamps.
The taste of
    your kiss
    is the prize
    of my collection.

Yours is a body
only a poet
could love
properly.

Dreaming
little dreams
in preparation
for dreaming
    huge
    impossible
    things.

She's a ghost,
but she stays with you,
haunts you,
protects you,
and loves you.
But she won't let you sleep.
She won't let you leave her.
And there's no place
you can go to be alone –
except Dimension X,
and let's be honest,
Dimension X ain't no picnic, either.

By the light of a candle,
a flickering weak orange light,
nothing special whatsoever happened.
No great love was expressed,
no vengeance sought or resolved,
no reunion or separation occurred.
But it was a pretty light
on a quiet night,
and nothing else mattered.

I will fall in love with you
tonight.
I will promise
gardens of flowers
with sculptures and fountains
and winding paths,
and I will mean
every word I say
with every ounce of my soul.
But I will fall in love
again
tomorrow night.
I will promise her
ribbons of silk
and saxophones
and jewel-encrusted masks,
and I will mean
every word I say
with every ounce of my soul.
But tonight,
tonight,
it's you.

If you
were my secret lover
I wouldn't even
tell you.
That's how close
I'd keep
our secret.

She looked at me
with diamonds
in her eyes
and razors
on her tongue,
but I was young
and it was night
and it was Paris.

If you can't see
beauty in me,
please lie.

You must first learn to say
all the things everyone else
has already said
before you can start
speaking your own truth.

I didn't save this place for you in my heart.
I didn't know the space was there till you filled it.

Did you ever think
you were
the most
beautiful
woman
ever?
You were right.

Tell me the story
of how you came
to be here
telling me stories.
I love that one.

Words are like that.

> They shift. They change.

> Their meanings alter with time.

Our intentions shift with age.

> The way we read changes.

>> The words become other words to other people.

The readers and the writers

> attach pre-conceptions and entire scenarios

> to words that appear to be otherwise innocent.

Words can be sneaky

> and they can be marvelous.

Death came for me. Five or six years back, she rode into town on a massively loud Harley. She held out her hand and said, "Let's ride."

"No."

I said nothing more. It was the equivalent of kicking and spitting and scratching for all I was worth. She removed her red helmet and smiled. Though her jacket was black and her gloves were black and her pants seriously so, her lips were as red as the helmet and her smile sincere. She winked at me and said, "I'll have my revenge."

A few weeks ago, my love and lover, the woman integral to all my plans for the future, succumbed to cancer. She died, and that night Death came to me again. I said, "You should've taken your revenge on me."

She smiled sadly and laid a single red rose on the bed where my partner had taken her last breath. "One day," Death said. "Today, I just wanted to offer my condolences."

DRAGON
by Mery-et Lescher

ACKNOWLEDGMENTS

This is not a book about how to heal. This isn't about how I healed – I'm not fully healed, not yet, maybe not ever. It's a snapshot of my healing process, but only in part, and only of a part of it. Not all the words were written after she died or even after she got sick. Most of the photos come from before. In a very real way, parts of this book have nothing to do with Mary. But make no mistake: the memory of her, the love we shared, and the life we lived pulse through this book like blood. I would never have put this together if things hadn't ended the way they had. I would've worked on something else, possibly a romantic fantasy set in Madrid. That was the plan. I'm not even sure it's possible now. But this book had to come out of me, these poems and these pictures, so I could move forward and work on anything else ever again. This was necessary for me. I'm not sure it was necessary for anyone else.

After Mary died, I wandered, and I spent time in Pennsylvania at the home of Brian Keene and Mary SanGiovanni, where I put this book together. I wrote some of the words and shot at least two of the photos there. They gave me a safe space to hide from the rest of the world, and I am grateful.

As always, a special thanks to Sabine and the Rose Fairy. You will always be with me.

PHOTOGRAPHY

All Photos Shot By John Urbancik
except Mary Lescher's portrait,
which was found at her parents' house

ABOUT THE PROJECT AND AUTHOR

John Urbancik's business card says *Writer. Photographer. Adventurer. Man.* Lately, he's been leaning heavily into the Adventurer part of that, hitting the road and wandering the United States like a nomad, vagabond, and tramp for the last half of 2019. As this is being written, and maybe by the time this is published, there is still no firm plan for what happens next. A good bet would be that more words will follow.

He was born on a small island in the northeast United States called Manhattan. He and his partner, Mary Lescher, had lived together in Orlando and Tallahassee, Florida; Sydney, Australia; Richmond, Virginia; and Madrid, Spain. The future, as ever, remains unwritten.

ALSO BY JOHN URBANCIK

NOVELS
Sins of Blood and Stone
Breath of the Moon
Once Upon a Time in Midnight
Stale Reality
The Corpse and the Girl from Miami
DarkWalker 1: Hunting Grounds
DarkWalker 2: Inferno
DarkWalker 3: The Deep City
DarkWalker 4: Armageddon

NOVELLAS
A Game of Colors
The Rise and Fall of Babylon (with Brian Keene)
Wings of the Butterfly
House of Shadow and Ash
Necropolis
Quicksilver
Beneath Midnight
Zombies vs. Aliens vs. Robots vs. Cowboys vs. Ninja vs.
Investment Bankers vs. Green Berets
Colette and the Tiger

COLLECTIONS
Shadows, Legends & Secrets
Sound and Vision
Tales of the Fantastic and the Phantasmagoric

NONFICTION
InkStained: On Creativity, Writing, and Art

INKSTAINS
Multiple volumes